The Six Nations Rugby Quiz Book

Matthew Jones

y Lolfa

First impression: 2012

© Copyright Matthew Jones and Y Lolfa Cyf., 2012

Cover design: Siôn Jones

ISBN: 978 184771 421 3

FSC

Published and printed in Wales
on paper from well maintained forests
by Y Lolfa Cyf., Talybont, Ceredigion SY24 5HE
website www.ylolfa.com
e-mail ylolfa@ylolfa.com
tel 01970 832 304
fax 832 782

Introduction

The Six Nations tournament conjures passion and rivalry between the biggest rugby countries in Europe. As February approaches, fans are busy making plans for a Max Boyce inspired Scottish trip, or have their flights booked for a journey to the Emerald Isle to drink plenty of the black stuff!

Cardiff is a sea of red set to a background chorus of 'Calon Lân', while Paris and Rome welcome those who struggle with the native language but still manage to share a story and a drink with an old adversary.

As kick-off approaches, the noise reverberates around Twickenham as thousands congregate in nervous anticipation. A fantastic competition. A supporters competition.

Here's an opportunity for you to think back to tournaments gone by – to try and remember who kicked that penalty? Or who scored that try? Was it Ronan O'Gara or Gregor Townsend who crossed that threshold first?

This book contains 50 rounds of 10 questions. Unless you are a dedicated rugby buff who watches Otley Seconds every weekend, it's unlikely that you will get them all correct, but the fun is in trying to think back and having a go at them! If you're on your way to a match while reading this, I hope your team wins!

Matthew Jones
January 2012

Questions

Round 1

1. **Stadio Flaminio is located in which city?**
   a. Bari
   b. Genoa
   c. Rome

2. **Shane Williams scored his 41st try on his 56th Welsh appearance making him his country's most successful finisher. Whose record did he break?**
   a. Ieuan Evans
   b. Gareth Thomas
   c. Gerald Davies

3. **If Richard Hill was the first, and Phillip de Glanville the second, who in 2008 became the third Bath player to captain England?**
   a. Lee Mears
   b. David Flatman
   c. Steve Borthwick

4. **Who in 2007 set an 83-cap Scotland record?**
   a. Dan Parks
   b. Jason White
   c. Scott Murray

5. **Who scored a try on his Irish Test debut against Scotland in 2000?**
   - a. Shane Horgan
   - b. Peter Stringer
   - c. John Hayes

6. **Former international flanker and coach Jean-Claude, is the father of which fly-half?**
   - a. David Skrela
   - b. Lionel Beauxis
   - c. Julien Peyrelongue

7. **At 18 years and 25 days, who became the youngest ever Six Nations international in 2010?**
   - a. Matthew Morgan
   - b. Tom Prydie
   - c. Steven Shingler

8. **With 114 English caps, who retired in 2004 as England's most experienced player?**

9. **Which Ulster outside-half scored 560 points in a 73-cap career for Ireland from 1996 to 2006?**

10. **Andy Leslie won 10 caps for New Zealand, all as captain during the 1970s. What's his link with the Six Nations?**

Round 2

1. **Who scored 400 points in 32 internationals from 1995 to 2004?**

    a. Paul Grayson
    b. Craig Chalmers
    c. Arwel Thomas

2. **What decision did Euan Murray make in 2009?**

    a. He would not play on Sundays due to religious beliefs
    b. Retire from international rugby
    c. Move to rugby league by signing for Wigan Warriors

3. **Which hooker won 98 French caps from 1996 to 2007?**

    a. Olivier Azam
    b. Raphaël Ibañez
    c. William Servat

4. **20 times capped Brett Sinkinson played for which club side?**

    a. Newport
    b. Cardiff
    c. Neath

5. **Which number 8 scored his first Six Nations try on his 28th tournament appearance in 2009?**

    a. Ryan Jones
    b. Sergio Parisse
    c. Simon Taylor

6. **Who made his 50th Irish appearance, against Wales, at Lansdowne Road in 2002?**

    a. Peter Clohessy
    b. Malcolm O'Kelly
    c. Keith Wood

7. **Who were the only team for reigning champions Wales to defeat in their 2006 Six Nations campaign?**

    a. Ireland
    b. England
    c. Scotland

8. **Lesley Vainikolo had played rugby league for which country prior to his England rugby union debut?**

9. **Which Scottish international stand-off joined London Welsh in 2009?**

10. **Who achieved back-to-back Six Nations championships in 2006 and 2007?**

Round 3

1. **What nationality is Maxime Médard?**
   - a. Italian
   - b. Scottish
   - c. French

2. **Who appeared in the 2007 BBC series *Strictly Come Dancing*?**
   - a. Kenny Logan
   - b. Andy Nicol
   - c. Shaun Longstaff

3. **Following 17 months of international retirement, who made a try scoring return for England in a 47–13 win over Wales in 2006?**
   - a. Martin Johnson
   - b. Lawrence Dallaglio
   - c. Neil Back

4. **Scott Gibbs won the inaugural Super League in 1996. Which club did he play for?**
   - a. Bradford Northern
   - b. St Helens
   - c. Wakefield Trinity

5. **How many seconds did it take for Rory Best to score Ireland's first try in their 9–19 victory over Wales in 2007?**
   - a. 25
   - b. 38
   - c. 47

6. **Who scored 113 points in 18 Six Nations matches from 2001 to 2007?**

    a. Ramiro Pez
    b. Cristian Stoica
    c. Gert Peens

7. **Zaire was the country of birth of which Frenchman?**

    a. Yannick Nyanga
    b. Olivier Brouzet
    c. Aurélien Rougerie

8. **Father and son, Alan and Rory both gained Scottish caps at scrum-half. What's the family surname?**

9. **Who became the youngest Welshman to gain 50 caps during Wales' 21–9 defeat by Scotland in 2007?**

10. **Who in 2008 became the first native West Indian to represent England?**

Round 4

1. **2001 saw a record 229 points scored by a team in the Six Nations. Which country set this record?**
   - a. England
   - b. Italy
   - c. France

2. **Which of these was not an international back-row forward?**
   - a. Julien Bonnaire
   - b. Patrick Tabacco
   - c. Damien Traille

3. **How many international points did Neil Jenkins score for Wales?**
   - a. 1,049
   - b. 1,364
   - c. 1,421

4. **Who skippered Italy 37 times from 2002 to 2007?**
   - a. Carlo Festuccia
   - b. Marco Bortolami
   - c. Cristian Stoica

5. **Who crushed England 43–13, with a 4-try haul in the 2007 Six Nations?**
   - a. France
   - b. Wales
   - c. Ireland

6.   **Marcus Di Rollo was named head coach of which club side in 2010?**

   a. Melrose
   b. Watsonians
   c. Currie

7.   **Who scored a hat-trick of tries in England's 43–22 victory over Scotland in 2005?**

   a. Jamie Noon
   b. Joe Worsley
   c. Steve Thompson

8.   **Which two countries have competed for the Calcutta Cup since 1879?**

9.   **During England's 2009 Six Nations championship, two players started at number 10. Name them.**

10. **Who captained Wales to a 2008 Grand Slam?**

Round 5

1. **Which London stadium is home to the England rugby team?**
    a. Wembley
    b. White Hart Lane
    c. Twickenham

2. **Ireland lost 17–20 to France in 2007. Who captained the side in Brian O'Driscoll's absence?**
    a. David Wallace
    b. Paul O'Connell
    c. Geordan Murphy

3. **With 6 touchdowns, who was Wales' top try scorer in their 2008 Grand Slam championship?**
    a. Shane Williams
    b. Mark Jones
    c. Martyn Williams

4. **Graeme Morrison made his Six Nations debut in 2009. Where was the Scottish international born?**
    a. Australia
    b. Hong Kong
    c. Namibia

5. **Who scored Italy's first Six Nations try on the 5th of February 2000?**
    a. Giampiero de Carli
    b. Carlo Orlandi
    c. Marco Rivaro

6. **Danny Cipriani played junior football for which side?**
    a. Glasgow Rangers
    b. Newcastle United
    c. Queens Park Rangers

7. **Which forward was the top try scorer in the 2004 Six Nations tournament?**
    a. Imanol Harinordoquy
    b. Dafydd Jones
    c. Keith Gleeson

8. **Prior to Brian O'Driscoll in 2009, who was the last Irish captain to win a Grand Slam?**

9. **Which Frenchman was known as the 'Grim Reaper'?**

10. **Which Welshman made a try-scoring debut for Toulon in their 38–10 victory over Stade Français in April 2011?**

Round 6

1. **Thom and Max Evans are cousins of which disc jockey?**
   a. Jo Whiley
   b. Chris Evans
   c. Chris Moyles

2. **With 50 points, who was the top scorer in the 2008 Six Nations?**
   a. Jonny Wilkinson
   b. Ceri Sweeney
   c. Mirco Bergamasco

3. **In which year was 'Flower of Scotland' first sung before an international?**
   a. 1970
   b. 1980
   c. 1990

4. **What role did Bernard Laporte take following his resignation as France's head coach?**
   a. TV pundit with Sky
   b. France's Secretary of State for sport
   c. Head coach of Bordeaux-Bègles

5. **Former Pontypridd second-row Bleddyn Davies is father to which international?**
   a. Jonathan Davies
   b. Bradley Davies
   c. Mefin Davies

6. **Who was the only Wales-based player in Ireland's 2009 Grand Slam winning team?**

      a. Tommy Bowe
      b. Simon Easterby
      c. Guy Easterby

7. **Which forward scored a brace of tries in Scotland's 22–27 win against Wales in 2002?**

      a. Scott Murray
      b. Gordon Bulloch
      c. Budge Pountney

8. **After 10 years of service, who left Gloucester in 2006 as their record England cap holder?**

9. **The Millennium Stadium is attached to which club ground?**

10. **Who was Scotland captain for their 2004 whitewash Six Nations season?**

Round 7

1. **Who was a team captain on the BBC's Saturday night series *Hole in the Wall*?**
    a. Gregor Townsend
    b. Austin Healey
    c. Rupert Moon

2. **Which of the following was the first to make a Six Nations debut?**
    a. James Hook
    b. Jamie Heaslip
    c. Ross Ford

3. **Which referee caused uproar at the end of Italy's 23–20 victory over Wales in 2007 by whistling for full time after telling Wales that there was time for a lineout?**
    a. Chris White
    b. Wayne Barnes
    c. Joël Jutge

4. **Who scored 5 of France's 9 tries in their 2001 Six Nations campaign?**
    a. Christophe Dominici
    b. Xavier Garbajosa
    c. Philippe Bernat-Salles

5. **In May 2010, who was named IRUPA Players' Player of the Year for the second time?**
    a. Keith Earls
    b. Tommy Bowe
    c. Jamie Heaslip

6. **Who made a try-scoring debut for Scotland in a 32–10 victory over Ireland in 2001?**
   a. Andrew Henderson
   b. Chris Cusiter
   c. Bruce Douglas

7. **Which future member of the Welsh coaching team played his last game for Cardiff Blues in May 2004, having to retire due to a knee injury at the age of 31?**
   a. Neil Jenkins
   b. Dan Baugh
   c. Robert Howley

8. **Which twice capped England scrum-half tragically died in Lanzarote at the age of 21 in 2003?**

9. **Which one time Italy coach scored 35 tries in 63 New Zealand Tests?**

10. **Playing at stand-off, who made the first of 32 Scottish appearances, against New Zealand in 1972?**

Round 8

1. **Dougie Hall, Fabio Ongaro and Jerry Flannery all started games in the 2006 Six Nations at which position?**
   a. Hooker
   b. Second-row
   c. Centre

2. **Bruce Douglas, Scott MacLeod and Sean Lamont have all played for which side?**
   a. Scarlets
   b. Ospreys
   c. Bridgend

3. **Matt Stevens received a two-year ban in 2009 after testing positive for which drug?**
   a. Tobacco
   b. Cocaine
   c. Aspirin

4. **Nick Mallett won 2 international caps, scoring a single try for which country?**
   a. England
   b. South Africa
   c. Namibia

5. **Who did Warren Gatland succeed as Ireland coach in 1998?**
   a. Dick Best
   b. Terry Holmes
   c. Brian Ashton

6. **Who scored 146 points in 13 Six Nations matches from 2000 to 2003?**

      a. Raphaël Ibañez

      b. Gérald Merceron

      c. Jean-Luc Sadourny

7. **Which rugby league side did Gareth Thomas join in 2010?**

      a. Crusaders

      b. St Helens

      c. Catalan Dragons

8. **In the first 10 years (2000–09) of the Six Nations, how many seasons did Jonny Wilkinson not make an appearance?**

9. **Who were the brothers that appeared together in the Irish front-row against Wales in 2006?**

10. **Who was Wales' ever-present starting scrum-half in their 2005 Grand Slam season?**

Round 9

1. **Marc Lièvremont became head coach of which country in 2007?**
   a. Wales
   b. Scotland
   c. France

2. *Finding my Feet* **was a 2004 autobiography by which dual code international?**
   a. Alan Tait
   b. Jason Robinson
   c. Allan Bateman

3. **Jonny Wilkinson's 29th drop-goal in 2008 was a world record. Who previously held the record?**
   a. Hugo Porta
   b. Michael Lynagh
   c. Grant Fox

4. **Who started all 5 games of Wales' 2005 Grand Slam tournament at hooker?**
   a. Robin McBryde
   b. Mefin Davies
   c. Barry Williams

5. **Which of the following was born in Townsville, Australia?**
   a. Ben Cohen
   b. Peter Stringer
   c. Luke McLean

6. **Who scored 29 tries in 62 internationals from 1997 to 2007?**

   a. Denis Hickie
   b. Geordan Murphy
   c. Girvan Dempsey

7. **Whose 101st appearance in 2011 made him Wales' most capped player?**

   a. Gethin Jenkins
   b. Matthew Rees
   c. Stephen Jones

8. **Which 2 countries have competed for the Giuseppe Garibaldi trophy since 2007?**

9. **Who contested the first Six Nations Friday night game in 2009?**

10. **Which future England rugby union international scored 3,115 points in 370 games for Wigan in rugby league?**

Round 10

1. **Which Irish hard man was known as 'The Claw'?**
    a. Anthony Foley
    b. Frankie Sheahan
    c. Peter Clohessy

2. **Which second-row became the last Coventry player to be capped by England in 1997?**
    a. Ben Kay
    b. Danny Grewcock
    c. Tim Rodber

3. **Miss Europe 2006 – Alexandra Rosenfeld, married which rugby player in 2010?**
    a. Morgan Stoddart
    b. Sergio Parisse
    c. Max Evans

4. **Tom Pearson's 119-year record as Wales' youngest debutant try scorer was broken in 2010. Who broke the record?**
    a. Josh Turnbull
    b. Tavis Knoyle
    c. George North

5. **Who in 2011 had to serve a 2-week ban for claiming referees in France's domestic competition are biased?**
    a. Yannick Jauzion
    b. Clément Poitrenaud
    c. Sébastien Chabal

6. **Aberdeen Wanderers was the breeding ground for which forward?**

      a. Bruce Douglas

      b. Allister Hogg

      c. Jason White

7. **Which of the following did not captain England?**

      a. Ben Cohen

      b. Kyran Bracken

      c. Dorian West

8. **Which Leinster player scored 20 points from 4 games in his debut Six Nations season in 2010?**

9. **What was Robert Howley the last to do in 1999, that David Young was the first to do in 2000?**

10. **Which country was the first to win consecutive Six Nations championships in 2000 and 2001?**

Round 11

1. **Paul O'Connell, Donncha O'Callaghan and Mick O'Driscoll are second-row forwards who have all played for which province?**
    - a. Munster
    - b. Leinster
    - c. Connacht

2. **During the 2008 Six Nations, what did Tom Shanklin, Ian Gough and Duncan Jones record?**
    - a. First international try
    - b. 50th cap
    - c. 2 tournament yellow cards

3. **Who won the last of 69 caps in Italy's maiden Six Nations match in March 2000?**
    - a. Roland de Marigny
    - b. Diego Dominguez
    - c. Massimo Cuttitta

4. **At the age of 23, Jonny Wilkinson became the youngest rugby union player to be awarded an MBE. Who at the age of 27 was the previous record holder?**
    - a. Barry John
    - b. Gareth Edwards
    - c. Jonathan Davies

5. **In which year was the Italian Rugby Federation formed?**
    a. 1928
    b. 1948
    c. 1968

6. **Philippe Bernat-Salles became the first player to do what in the Six Nations during the 2001 season?**
    a. Receive a red card
    b. Score a try in all 5 of his team's matches
    c. Kick 3 drop-goals in a game

7. **Who worked for a window firm, in a bakery, as a building site labourer and in a job centre before becoming a professional rugby player?**
    a. Mike Tindall
    b. Keith Wood
    c. Shane Williams

8. **Who scored 4 tries for England against Italy in 2011?**

9. **Andy Robinson spent his playing days with which club?**

10. **Who starred in Channel 5's 2011 series *The Batchelor*?**

Round 12

1. **In which city was the former Lansdowne Road stadium?**
    - a. Belfast
    - b. Cork
    - c. Dublin

2. **Which former Scottish scrum-half was appointed Gloucester head coach in 2009?**
    - a. Andy Nicol
    - b. Bryan Redpath
    - c. Gary Armstrong

3. **Gareth Thomas' 93rd cap in 2007 made him Wales' most capped international. Whose record did he break?**
    - a. Gareth Llewellyn
    - b. Robert Jones
    - c. Ieuan Evans

4. **Future England prop Duncan Bell snubbed the England A side in 2004, as he wanted to play for which country under residency rules?**
    - a. Scotland
    - b. Ireland
    - c. Wales

5. **Who scored an Italian try against Scotland in 2007 with only 19 seconds on the clock?**

   a. Mauro Bergamasco
   b. Kaine Robertson
   c. Andrea Masi

6. **France international footballer, William Gallas, is the cousin of which rugby player?**

   a. François Trinh-Duc
   b. Thierry Dusautoir
   c. Mathieu Bastareaud

7. **During the 2010 Six Nations, who was England's only back-row forward to start all 5 matches?**

   a. Nick Easter
   b. Lewis Moody
   c. James Haskell

8. **Who were the 3 Ireland captains during the 2002 Six Nations?**

9. **Strettle, Wallace and Marty. What is their first name?**

10. **With 44 points, who were Wales' 2 joint top points scorers in their 2008 Grand Slam campaign?**

Round 13

1. **Ireland's 2009 Grand Slam was their first in how many years?**
   - a. 41
   - b. 51
   - c. 61

2. **Who scored his first international try in Wales' 24–16 victory over Italy in 2011?**
   - a. Sam Warburton
   - b. Rob McCusker
   - c. Andy Powell

3. **Which future England international won the 1999 under-19s World Cup with New Zealand?**
   - a. Lesley Vainikolo
   - b. Riki Flutey
   - c. Andy Goode

4. **Which country was Morgan Parra talking about in 2009 when he said they 'cheat every weekend'?**
   - a. England
   - b. Wales
   - c. Ireland

5. **Who captained Italy in their maiden Six Nations championship?**
   - a. Alessandro Troncon
   - b. Diego Dominguez
   - c. Carlo Checchinato

6. **Who against Italy in 2011 became the 25th Welshman to win his 50th cap?**

   a. Jamie Robinson

   b. James Hook

   c. Lee Byrne

7. **In 2002, who became the first Scot to be sent off in a Test match?**

   a. Gavin Kerr

   b. Stuart Grimes

   c. Nathan Hines

8. **Who scored a French hat-trick in their 26–21 victory against Ireland in 2008?**

9. **The inaugural Six Nations championship occurred in 2000. Who became the first winners?**

10. **Which Italian back-row forward scored a try on his 75th appearance, in his country's 24–16 loss to Wales in 2011?**

Round 14

1. **Which of the following has not played scrum-half for Italy?**

   a. Tito Tebaldi

   b. Pietro Travagli

   c. Robert Howley

2. **2002 saw the first Six Nations Grand Slam. Who achieved this?**

   a. France

   b. Italy

   c. Scotland

3. **What type of vehicle was Andy Powell driving when charged with drink driving in 2010?**

   a. Tractor

   b. Golf buggy

   c. Horse and cart

4. ***Where we go from here* was a 2010 album, released by which forward?**

   a. Denis Leamy

   b. Ian Gough

   c. Andrew Sheridan

5. **Which Scotland hooker began his career with Biggar RFC?**

   a. Scott Lawson

   b. Dougie Hall

   c. Robbie Russell

6. **Who did Alan Phillips succeed as Wales's team manager in 2002?**

   a. Robert Norster
   b. David Pickering
   c. Derwyn Jones

7. **Which Leinster man made his first Six Nations start in 7 years, against Italy in 2010?**

   a. Kevin McLaughlin
   b. Malcolm O'Kelly
   c. Leo Cullen

8. **What did James Brent-Wood design?**

9. **Which son of a former Welsh international coach captained Ireland to the 2009/10 under-20s Six Nations championship?**

10. **Whose final international match in 2000 left him as Wales' most capped hooker with 58 appearances?**

Round 15

1. **Which Irishman joined Ben Cohen and Austin Healey as joint top try scorer with 5, in the 2000 Six Nations?**
    a. Shane Horgan
    b. Denis Hickie
    c. Brian O'Driscoll

2. **Craig Gower played rugby league for which country before becoming a union international with Italy?**
    a. New Zealand
    b. Australia
    c. Papua New Guinea

3. **Which Scottish forward shares the same first name as the lead singer of the Stereophonics?**
    a. Kelly Brown
    b. David Callam
    c. Euan Murray

4. **Prior to Jason Robinson's appearance as captain in 2004, who was the last Sale man to lead England?**
    a. Eric Evans
    b. Fran Cotton
    c. Steve Smith

5. **Welsh national anthem composers and writers, Evan and James James, were from which town?**
    a. Newbridge
    b. Ammanford
    c. Pontypridd

6. **In 2011, who made a record 200th appearance for Leinster?**

   a. Shane Horgan
   b. Leo Cullen
   c. Gordon D'Arcy

7. **Squash great Jonah Barrington is the godfather of which international?**

   a. Andrew Trimble
   b. Nick Easter
   c. Carlo Festuccia

8. **Which scrum-half started all 5 of England's 2011 Six Nations games?**

9. **Which 2 countries have competed for the Millennium Trophy since 1988?**

10. **Who were the 2 internationals suspended by London Wasps in April 2011 following a brawl at a London pub?**

Round 16

1. **How many championship points are awarded for a win in the Six Nations tournament?**
    a. 2
    b. 3
    c. 4

2. **In 2003, a rugby union coach won the BBC Sports Personality of the Year coach award, for the first time. Who was awarded the accolade?**
    a. Dick Best
    b. Clive Woodward
    c. Gareth Jenkins

3. **Who did Italy defeat in 2007 to claim their first away Six Nations win?**
    a. England
    b. Wales
    c. Scotland

4. **Who made a try-scoring debut against Ireland in 2005?**
    a. Benoît Baby
    b. Mark Jones
    c. Andrew Henderson

5. **In 1998, which future England front-row forward joined Bridgend following a stint in New Zealand?**
    a. Phil Greening
    b. Julian White
    c. David Flatman

6. **Jim Hamilton set a record for Scotland in 2006 which Michael Owen did for Wales in 2002. What was this?**
   a. Youngest captain
   b. First forward to score an international try hat-trick
   c. 1,000th capped player

7. **Against Ulster in 2010, who became the first player to make 150 appearances in an Ospreys jersey?**
   a. Paul James
   b. Sonny Parker
   c. Lee Byrne

8. **On retiring, Martin Johnson had captained England 39 times. Whose 59-match record was he unable to better?**

9. **Which Irishman was IRB Player of the Year in 2001?**

10. **Did Iestyn Harris win a greater number of Welsh rugby union or rugby league caps?**

Round 17

1. **In which city would you find Stade de France?**
   a. Nice
   b. Paris
   c. Lille

2. **What were Ospreys players banned from doing in 2011?**
   a. Wearing fake tan
   b. Eating beefburgers
   c. Growing beards

3. **Which English second-row racked up 44 weeks of suspensions during his career?**
   a. Martin Johnson
   b. Steve Borthwick
   c. Danny Grewcock

4. **Roland de Marigny did not play for which of the following?**
   a. Llanelli
   b. Bangor
   c. Swansea

5. **Who won a single rugby league cap before earning 30 union caps and scoring 6 tries for Scotland?**
   a. James McLaren
   b. Glenn Metcalfe
   c. Jamie Mayer

6. **Which prop made his debut at the age of 27 in 1996, going on to make a further 38 appearances, until his last in 2004?**
    a. Jean-Jacques Crenca
    b. Spencer John
    c. Paul Wallace

7. **Magnus Lund's father Morten was a Norwegian international. What sport did he play?**
    a. Football
    b. Basketball
    c. Ice Hockey

8. **Who coached Ireland to a 2009 Grand Slam?**

9. **Who made a try-scoring debut for Toulon against Stade Français at the end of the 2010/11 season?**

10. **Who in 1998 became the first Northampton player since Robert Taylor in 1970 to captain England?**

Round 18

1. **What position would you associate with Pascal Papé, Luke Charteris and Paul O'Connell?**
    - a. Second-row
    - b. Prop
    - c. Full-back

2. **Tokoroa, New Zealand, was the birthplace of which Irish scrum-half?**
    - a. Eoin Reddan
    - b. Isaac Boss
    - c. Peter Stringer

3. **Who scored all 19 points as Scotland defeated England 19–13 in 2000?**
    - a. Craig Chalmers
    - b. Gregor Townsend
    - c. Duncan Hodge

4. **In which year did Andy Titterrell make his only 2 Six Nations appearances?**
    - a. 2001
    - b. 2005
    - c. 2009

5. **Who was voted Wales' sexiest man in 2006?**
    - a. Ryan Jones
    - b. Lee Byrne
    - c. Ian Gough

6. **How many minutes did it take for Italy to build a 21–0 lead against Scotland in 2007?**

    a. 6
    b. 16
    c. 26

7. **Which front-row forward made his Six Nations debut as a substitute against Ireland in 2005?**

    a. Nicolas Mas
    b. Fabien Barcella
    c. Dimitri Szarzewski

8. **What did Scotland win in 2006 for the first time since 2000?**

9. **Name the former England captain whose middle names are Bruno Nero.**

10. **Who was the New Zealand try-scoring hooker, in their 37–22 victory over Swansea in 1989?**

Round 19

1. **Craig and Scott are the sons of which former international?**
   a. Gareth Edwards
   b. Derek Quinnell
   c. John Taylor

2. **Bernard Jackman and Keith Wood are known for playing at which position?**
   a. Wing
   b. Scrum-half
   c. Hooker

3. **Who was controversially appointed Scotland's first foreign coach, but only lasted 17 games with 3 wins?**
   a. Matt Williams
   b. Jason Little
   c. David Campese

4. **Who scored 12 tries in a 52-cap career from 1994 to 2005?**
   a. Craig Morgan
   b. Rupert Moon
   c. Mark Taylor

5. **Who scored Italy's second ever Six Nations try in a 47–16 loss to Wales in 2000?**
   a. Wilhelmus Visser
   b. Tino Paoletti
   c. Marco Rivaro

6. **With 6 tries, who was top try scorer in the 2001 Six Nations?**

    a. Dan Luger
    b. Iain Balshaw
    c. Will Greenwood

7. **Which Six Nations star in 2010 became the first player to win 4 European Cups?**

    a. John Hayes
    b. Stephen Jones
    c. Cédric Heymans

8. **Ireland won their first Triple Crown since 1985 in 2004. Who was man of the tournament?**

9. **Who moved to Brive in 2009 having previously scored 55 tries in 241 Newcastle Falcons appearances?**

10. **Which country has Dimitri Yachvili's brother Grégoire played for?**

Round 20

1. **Which side gave Andy Robinson his first role in rugby following his 2006 sacking by England?**
   - a. Neath
   - b. Edinburgh
   - c. London Scottish

2. **Which Frenchman spent 5 years with Sale Sharks from 2004 to 2009?**
   - a. Sébastien Chabal
   - b. Jérôme Thion
   - c. Frédéric Michalak

3. **Iestyn, Jonathan and Rhys are Welsh internationals who share which surname?**
   - a. Morgan
   - b. Norster
   - c. Thomas

4. **Who scored Ireland's last ever try at Lansdowne Road in a 31–5 victory over Wales in 2006?**
   - a. Denis Hickie
   - b. Peter Stringer
   - c. Girvan Dempsey

5. **In 2002, who became the first Gloucester player to captain England?**
   - a. Trevor Woodman
   - b. Henry Paul
   - c. Phil Vickery

6. **Dan Parks' initial foray in British rugby was a 6-game stint in 2001. Which club did he represent?**
    a. Leeds Tykes
    b. Aberavon
    c. Watsonians

7. **Where was Gonzalo Garcia born?**
    a. Mendoza, Argentina
    b. Los Angeles, USA
    c. Freetown, Sierra Leone

8. **Jim Renwick, Colin Deans and Tony Stanger were taught physical education in Hawick by which broadcasting legend?**

9. **Which future member of the Welsh coaching team was Welsh Player of the Year in both 1996 and 1997?**

10. **Who lost 9 of his 16 games as England captain under the management of Andy Robinson?**

Round 21

1. **Guilhem Guirado, Richard Hibbard and Leonardo Ghiraldini are known for playing at which position?**
    a. Hooker
    b. Flanker
    c. Number 8

2. **Which of the following is a France international?**
    a. Tommaso Reato
    b. Leigh Halfpenny
    c. Julien Malzieu

3. **Where is Stadio Beltrametti located?**
    a. Piacenza
    b. Worcester
    c. Swansea

4. **Who defeated England 15–9 in 2008 to record their only Six Nations win of the season?**
    a. Italy
    b. Scotland
    c. Wales

5. **Malcolm O'Kelly set a 70-cap Irish record in a match against Scotland in 2005. Who was the previous record holder?**
    a. Mike Gibson
    b. Tony O'Reilly
    c. Fergus Slattery

6. **Following England's 24–13 victory in Paris in 2008, whom did Marc Lièvremont describe as a 'grotesque clown'?**
   a. James Haskell
   b. Mike Tindall
   c. Mark Regan

7. **Who were the 3 players to score points in Scotland's 15–15 draw with England in 2010?**
   a. Dan Parks, Jonny Wilkinson and Toby Flood
   b. Chris Paterson, Kelly Brown and Jonny Wilkinson
   c. Chris Paterson, Dan Parks and Phil Godman

8. **Name the first Newport Gwent Dragon to captain Wales.**

9. **Who was England's only ever-present back-rower in their first 5 seasons (2000–04) of the Six Nations?**

10. **Scotland recorded a surprise 20–16 victory over France in 2006. Who scored their 2 tries?**

Round 22

1. Which countrymen are called the 'Azzurri'?

    a. English

    b. Italians

    c. Welsh

2. Which of the following was inducted into the IRB Hall of Fame in 2003?

    a. Jo Maso

    b. Gareth Jenkins

    c. Frank Hadden

3. The Recreation Ground is home to which side?

    a. Aironi

    b. Ospreys

    c. Bath

4. Exeter Chiefs signed which Welsh prop in 2011?

    a. Craig Mitchell

    b. Rhys Thomas

    c. Chris Horsman

5. Due to conflicting medical opinion, which Scotsman was limited to a single minute of play for Toulouse in the 2007/08 season?

    a. Andrew Henderson

    b. Hugo Southwell

    c. Marcus Di Rollo

6. **Who scored Ireland's only try in their 19–13 victory over England in 2005?**

    a. Denis Hickie
    b. Brian O'Driscoll
    c. Marcus Horan

7. **Which Scottish international married TV presenter Gabby Yorath in 2001?**

    a. Kenny Logan
    b. Budge Pountney
    c. Stuart Grimes

8. **In 1999, who was appointed the first professional head coach of France?**

9. **On March 10th 2007, who scored all of Ireland's points as they beat Scotland 19–18 to achieve a Triple Crown?**

10. **In 2004, who became the first former rugby league international to captain the England rugby union side?**

Round 23

1. **Who was the only Wallace brother to achieve over 50 caps for Ireland?**
    a. Richard
    b. Paul
    c. David

2. **The singer Charlotte Church split with her fiancé in June 2010. Who was he?**
    a. Ben Evans
    b. Ceri Sweeney
    c. Gavin Henson

3. **Where would you find Stadio Santa Rosa?**
    a. Cagliari
    b. Cross Keys
    c. Clydebank

4. **England's then most capped full-back, retired at the age of 30 in 2007. Who was this Bath player?**
    a. Iain Balshaw
    b. Matt Perry
    c. Jason Robinson

5. **During the 2008 Six Nations, which Australian-born second-row became the 23rd player to win 50 Scottish caps?**
    a. Stuart Grimes
    b. Nathan Hines
    c. Scott MacLeod

6. *Half Time*, a 2009 autobiography, was by which international referee?

   a. George Clancy
   b. Wayne Barnes
   c. Nigel Owens

7. In 2010, who kicked a drop-goal after 3 minutes of play, as France defeated England 12–10 in a Grand Slam winning seaon?

   a. François Trinh-Duc
   b. Morgan Parra
   c. Dimitri Yachvili

8. Who was the first Welsh captain to physically lift a Triple Crown trophy?

9. Who started as Ireland's full-back in all 5 of their 2009 Grand Slam winning games?

10. Stuart Abbott and Carlo Del Fava were born in which country?

Round 24

1. **In 2001, a team in the Six Nations scored a tournament record 29 tries. Which country achieved this?**

   a. Italy

   b. England

   c. Scotland

2. **Fabien Pelous became France's most capped player when he won his 112th cap in 2007. Whose record did he beat?**

   a. Philippe Sella

   b. Serge Blanco

   c. Jean-Pierre Rives

3. **Who became the first Italian to win 100 caps?**

   a. Santiago Dellapè

   b. Mauro Bergamasco

   c. Alessandro Troncon

4. **How is Roy Williamson of the folk group The Corries associated with the Six Nations?**

   a. Wrote 'Flower of Scotland'

   b. Was president of the SRU from 2001 until 2009

   c. Performed at the opening ceremony of the Aviva Stadium

5. **Who celebrated his retirement with a testimonial match with a selected side against a Jason Leonard side at the Millennium Stadium in 2004?**

    a. Scott Quinnell

    b. Neil Jenkins

    c. Ieuan Evans

6. **In 2003, who became the first Irishman since Tom McKinney in 1957 to earn a Great Britain rugby league cap?**

    a. Brian Carney

    b. Girvan Dempsey

    c. Denis Hickie

7. **What's the non-rugby link between Andy Goode and Matt Mullen?**

    a. Half-brothers

    b. Worked together as gardeners

    c. Goode was Mullen's babysitter when young

8. **In 2011, who became Wales' second youngest captain after Gareth Edwards?**

9. **Sylvain Marconnet became France's most capped prop in 2007. Whose record did he break?**

10. **Who in 2008 broke Gavin Hastings' 667 points Scotland record?**

Round 25

1. **Murrayfield Stadium is found in which city?**
   - a. Aberdeen
   - b. Edinburgh
   - c. Glasgow

2. **Which club did Shaun Edwards sign for on his 17th birthday for £35,000?**
   - a. Widnes
   - b. Halifax
   - c. Wigan

3. **Which of the following was born in Mar del Plata, Argentina?**
   - a. Lawrence Dallaglio
   - b. Sergio Parisse
   - c. Scott Quinnell

4. **How many of Josh Lewsey's 55 caps were at outside-half?**
   - a. 0
   - b. 2
   - c. 4

5. **Which Frenchman was awarded the IRPA special merit award for services to rugby in 2007?**
   - a. Fabien Pelous
   - b. Aurélien Rougerie
   - c. Christophe Dominici

6. **At the 20th attempt, Italy won their first away Six Nations match in 2007. Who were the opposition?**

    a. Wales
    b. France
    c. Scotland

7. **Why did Martin Johnson miss the 2000 Six Nations?**

    a. 12-week suspension for a fight at club level with Chris Wyatt
    b. Contracted to play for Auckland Blues
    c. Achilles tendon injury

8. **Why were certain games of the 2001 Six Nations championship postponed until September and October of that year?**

9. **ITV's 2009 daytime quiz show *The Fuse* was presented by which former England international?**

10. **Which Scottish second-row was cleared twice – once in 2008 and once in 2009 – for failing drugs tests, the first due to asthma medication and the second due to alcohol?**

Round 26

1. **Which of these was an Irish international?**
   a. Luca Martin
   b. Michael Mullins
   c. Gareth Cooper

2. **In which year did Italy record their first 2 victories in a Six Nations season?**
   a. 2004
   b. 2006
   c. 2007

3. **Which French side signed Mike Phillips in 2011?**
   a. Stade Français
   b. Bayonne
   c. Perpignan

4. **John Barclay and Graeme Morrison were both born in which part of Asia?**
   a. Hong Kong
   b. Macau
   c. Singapore

5. **Scotland lost 24–31 to France in 2011. Who scored a try on his debut as captain?**
   a. Alastair Kellock
   b. Dougie Hall
   c. Jason White

6. **How many international rugby league caps did Gareth Thomas earn for Wales?**

      a. 0

      b. 2

      c. 4

7. **Former Italian coach, Brad Johnstone, won 13 New Zealand caps. Which position did he play?**

      a. Prop

      b. Flanker

      c. Number 8

8. **Who was the Irish scrum-half that scored 16 tries in 106 appearances for London Wasps during a 4-year period starting in 2005?**

9. **Who was called Welsh rugby's 'Great Redeemer'?**

10. **Cricketer Mark Ramprakash won the 2006 BBC series of *Strictly Come Dancing*. Which former rugby international came second?**

Round 27

1. **Which of these was a Scottish second-row?**

   a. Xavier Garbajosa

   b. Rupert Moon

   c. Richard Metcalfe

2. **Which future Italian coach, in 1992, became the first All Black to reach the 50-Test milestone?**

   a. Zinzan Brooke

   b. John Kirwan

   c. Sean Fitzpatrick

3. **In 2009, who became the first Englishman to coach Scotland?**

   a. Ben Clarke

   b. Andy Robinson

   c. Dean Richards

4. **Which of the following has an engineering degree?**

   a. Stephen Jones

   b. Craig Gower

   c. Thomas Castaignède

5. **What was controversial about Tommy Bowe's try in Ireland's 26–16 victory over Italy in 2006?**

   a. His foot was in touch

   b. He didn't ground the ball correctly

   c. Ronan O'Gara's pass was forward

6. **What did Mike Catt do in 2007 that Charles Jacobs did in 1964 and Ivor Preece did in 1949?**
   a. Scored a hat-trick of tries against Wales
   b. Won his inaugural game as captain, against France
   c. Broke his arm during a match but played on until the end

7. **Scott Gibbs did not play for which of the following?**
   a. Cardiff
   b. Neath
   c. Swansea

8. **Simon Danielli moved to Ireland in 2007 following the disbandment of the Border Reivers. Which province did he join?**

9. **Who lied in 2009, saying he'd been assaulted while returning to his hotel in New Zealand, even though he'd actually had a fight with a teammate?**

10. **Welsh television presenter Sarra Elgan is married to which former Irish international?**

Round 28

1. Serge Betsen played 17 years for which club side?

    a. Biarritz

    b. Swansea

    c. London Wasps

2. Which of these has played prop for Wales?

    a. Darren Morris

    b. Chris Wyatt

    c. Geraint Lewis

3. Jonny Wilkinson captained the England senior side for the first time in 2003. This made him the first representative of which club to do so?

    a. West Hartlepool

    b. Newcastle Falcons

    c. Birkenhead Park

4. Chris Paterson created which record in February 2010?

    a. First Scottish player to score 1,000 international points

    b. First Scotsman to earn 100 caps

    c. Oldest player to score a Six Nations try

5. Who kicked a last minute penalty in a 20–23 victory in 2010, preventing Ireland from a Triple Crown?

    a. Toby Flood

    b. James Hook

    c. Dan Parks

6. **Who in 2003 became Italy's youngest ever captain?**
   a. Santiago Dellapè
   b. Aaron Persico
   c. Marco Bortolami

7. **Which dual code international was known as 'The Clamp'?**
   a. Allan Bateman
   b. David Young
   c. John Bentley

8. **In which country would you find Stadio Comunale San Vito?**

9. **Which New Zealand-born centre won 21 French caps from 2001 to 2004?**

10. **Which Munster legend played the last of his 62 international Tests, against Wales in 2005, and had a father, Brendan, who also played for Ireland?**

Round 29

1. **Which of the following would you associate with a trademark beard?**
   a. Sébastien Chabal
   b. Paul Wallace
   c. Toby Flood

2. **Which of the following was a Scottish international?**
   a. Denis Dallan
   b. Cameron Murray
   c. David Auradou

3. **Martin Corry won 64 England caps. How many of these were Six Nations starts?**
   a. 5
   b. 15
   c. 25

4. **Who made his Test debut in 2003, but then had to wait 6 years before gaining his second?**
   a. Lee Byrne
   b. Adam Jones
   c. Paul James

5. **Which of the following has played in the front, second and back-row during his career with Bristol?**
   a. Andrew Sheridan
   b. Robert Sidoli
   c. Simon Danielli

6. Ireland defeated England 28–24 at Twickenham in 2006 thanks to a dramatic 78th minute touchdown. Who scored the try?

    a. Andrew Trimble
    b. Denis Leamy
    c. Shane Horgan

7. Who scored Italy's only try in their 2004 victory over Scotland?

    a. Andrea de Rossi
    b. Fabio Ongaro
    c. Carlo Festuccia

8. Jamie Roberts made his international debut against Scotland in 2008. Which position was he selected at?

9. Who are the owners of Croke Park?

10. Caledonia Reds appointed which future international coach as their assistant coach in 1997?

Round 30

1. **Who resigned as England manager in November 2011 following 38 games in charge?**
   a. Martin Johnson
   b. Brian Moore
   c. Rob Andrew

2. **Which of the following has played full-back for Scotland?**
   a. Brent Cockbain
   b. Ben Hinshelwood
   c. Nicolas Brusque

3. **The Welsh Rugby Union announced a 3-year shirt sponsorship deal in 2010. Which company became emblazoned on their shirt?**
   a. Admiral
   b. General
   c. Major

4. **Who bravely missed a 50-metre penalty kick in the final seconds of Wales' encounter with Ireland in 2009 to present the Irish with a Grand Slam?**
   a. James Hook
   b. Leigh Halfpenny
   c. Stephen Jones

5. **Martin Castrogiovanni's junior basketball career was ended by which event?**

    a. A national ban in Argentina on American sports
    b. He punched a referee
    c. Hugo Porta visited his school and set up a rugby academy

6. **Who scored a try after 43 seconds to set the scene for a 31–6 French victory over England in 2006?**

    a. Jérôme Thion
    b. Aurélien Rougerie
    c. Florian Fritz

7. **Duncan Bell signed his first professional contract in 1996 with Ebbw Vale. How much was he paid?**

    a. £100 per game plus accommodation
    b. £300 per game plus £50 per win
    c. £1,000 per week

8. **What was historic about Ireland's game against France on Sunday, 13th of February 2011?**

9. **Lloyd Williams is the son of which British and Irish Lion?**

10. **The USA appointed which former Six Nations coach as their head coach in 2009?**

Round 31

1. **Which former English prop shares his name with a celebrity chef?**
   a. Graham Rowntree
   b. Julian White
   c. Phil Vickery

2. **Which of these has not been capped as a second-row?**
   a. James Hamilton
   b. Paul Griffen
   c. Alun Wyn Jones

3. **Which Glasgow Warriors star opted to join Sale Sharks in the summer of 2012?**
   a. Duncan Weir
   b. Ruaridh Jackson
   c. Richie Gray

4. **Footballer Ryan Giggs won the BBC Wales 2009 Sports Personality of the Year award. The cyclist Geraint Thomas came second, but who came third?**
   a. Rhys Priestland
   b. Jamie Roberts
   c. Morgan Stoddart

5. **Serge Betsen was born in which country?**
   a. Mexico
   b. Nigeria
   c. Cameroon

6. **How did Ronan O'Gara in 2009 emulate Jack Kyle's feat in 1948?**
   a. Played every game at fly-half in a Grand Slam winning side
   b. Scored 500 international points
   c. Kicked a drop-goal in 5 consecutive internationals

7. **Who scored Italy's 7 points in their 20–7 defeat by England in 2007?**
   a. Kaine Robertson
   b. Andrea Scanavacca
   c. Roland de Marigny

8. **1966 football World Cup winner George Cohen is the uncle of which rugby international?**

9. **Which former Widnes Vikings rugby league player, went on to win 23 rugby union caps for Scotland, scoring 2 tries in their 2005 Six Nations campaign?**

10. **Who won his 100th international cap in Ireland's 27–12 victory over Wales in 2010?**

Round 32

1. **Which of these was an Italian prop?**
   a. Carlos Nieto
   b. Phil Godman
   c. Ian Gough

2. **Which of the following was not born in England?**
   a. Shontayne Hape
   b. Max Evans
   c. Luke Charteris

3. **Who won 4 Grand Slams in a 90-Test career from 1997 to 2007?**
   a. Will Greenwood
   b. Olivier Magne
   c. Chris Wyatt

4. **Kevin Morgan, Martyn Williams and Shane Williams were Wales' joint top try scorers in their 2005 Grand Slam season. How many tries did they each score?**
   a. 3
   b. 4
   c. 5

5. **A Dan Parks drop-goal gave Scotland a 20–23 victory on March 20th 2010. Who did they defeat, preventing a Triple Crown?**
   a. Wales
   b. England
   c. Ireland

6. **Who scored a brace of tries in Ireland's 27–12 win over Wales in 2010?**
    a. Jamie Heaslip
    b. Keith Earls
    c. Tomás O'Leary

7. **Pieter Le Roux, a springbok flanker in the early 20th century was the great-grandfather of which Six Nations player?**
    a. Nick Easter
    b. Santiago Dellapè
    c. Adam Jones

8. **Who became Ulster coach in December 2007?**

9. **In 2010, who became the first player to score 50 tries in an Ospreys jersey?**

10. **Irish front-row forwards Keith Wood and Mike Ross have both played for which London club?**

Round 33

1. **Raphaël Ibañez finished his career at which club?**
   a. London Wasps
   b. Ospreys
   c. Ulster

2. **What was Shaun Perry's occupation before becoming a professional rugby player?**
   a. Accountant
   b. Hairdresser
   c. Welder

3. **Todd Blackadder was named Crusaders head coach in 2008. He had previously held the position of assistant coach with which country?**
   a. Italy
   b. Scotland
   c. France

4. **Which club did James Hook join in 2011?**
   a. Perpignan
   b. Bourgoin
   c. La Rochelle

5. **Who started at scrum-half for Italy against England in 2009?**
   a. Sergio Parisse
   b. Salvatore Perugini
   c. Mauro Bergamasco

6. **Dubarry Park, Athlone, is the home to which club side?**
   a. Corinthians
   b. Buccaneers
   c. Bruff

7. **Who was Scotland's ever-present outside-half during the 2009 Six Nations?**
   a. Colin Gregor
   b. Phil Godman
   c. Ruaridh Jackson

8. **Who finished his Wales career in 2007 as his country's most capped forward with 94 appearances?**

9. **Marco Bortolami played for which English side from 2006 to 2010?**

10. **Which future England international spent 4 days in a Rosario prison cell while on a tour of Argentina with Wellington Academy in 2001?**

Round 34

1. **Tommy Bowe, Nikki Walker and Shane Williams have played for which Welsh side?**
   a. Cross Keys
   b. Ospreys
   c. Newport

2. **Moray Low, Gavin Kerr and Mattie Stewart have all appeared for Scotland at which position?**
   a. Prop
   b. Number 8
   c. Wing

3. **What's the surname of the internationally capped father and son pair – Claude and Richard?**
   a. Lombard
   b. Dourthe
   c. Brouzet

4. **Warren Gatland made a record 140 appearances for a New Zealand province from 1986 to 1994. Which one?**
   a. Waikato
   b. Otago
   c. Auckland

5. **Which forward scored 2 tries in England's 2010 victory over Wales?**
   a. David Wilson
   b. Steve Borthwick
   c. James Haskell

6. **Who scored Italy's third ever Six Nations try, in a 60–13 loss to Ireland in March 2000?**

    a. Mauro Bergamasco
    b. Andrea Gritti
    c. Andrea De Rossi

7. **Who played for Australia under-19 and under-21 teams before making his Ireland debut in 2002?**

    a. Keith Gleeson
    b. Eric Miller
    c. Gary Longwell

8. **Which England international has a brother Erik who has been capped by Norway?**

9. **Who succeeded Graham Henry as Wales' head coach in 2002?**

10. **Who made 54 consecutive appearances in the Six Nations for Ireland from 2000 to 2010?**

Round 35

1. Which of these was an Italian international?

    a. Giovanni Raineri

    b. Michael Lynagh

    c. Frank Bunce

2. Thomas Castaignède spent 7 seasons in English rugby. Which club did he play for?

    a. Preston Grasshoppers

    b. Bath

    c. Saracens

3. Chris Anthony, Spencer John and Peter Rogers were Welsh internationals that played at which position?

    a. Hooker

    b. Prop

    c. Flanker

4. Where's McDiarmid Park?

    a. Edinburgh

    b. Perth

    c. Aberdeen

5. Which of the following is a qualified helicopter pilot?

    a. Stephen Jones

    b. Rory Lawson

    c. Ben Cohen

6. **How did Leo Cullen make Irish history in 2011?**

   a. First Leinster player to make 50 Six Nations appearances
   b. First Irish international to become a Member of Parliament
   c. 100th man to captain Ireland

7. **Who was the opposition when Pablo Canavosio scored the only try of the game as Italy won 16–12 in February 2010?**

   a. Scotland
   b. Ireland
   c. England

8. **What has Matt Dawson got in common with Cliff Morgan, Gareth Edwards and Bill Beaumont?**

9. **Who were the all-Ospreys front-row to finish the game for Wales against Italy in 2011?**

10. **Against France in 2009, who became the 20th pair of brothers to appear in the same Scotland side?**

Round 36

1. **Who are known as 'Les Bleus'?**
    a. Ireland
    b. Scotland
    c. France

2. **Which hooker played his last international in 2003 having amassed 15 tries in 58 matches?**
    a. Keith Wood
    b. Andrew Lamerton
    c. Richard Cockerill

3. **Toby Faletau's father Kili played international rugby for which country?**
    a. Fiji
    b. Tonga
    c. Namibia

4. **How many games did Lawrence Dallaglio win out of his 22 in charge of England?**
    a. 10
    b. 12
    c. 14

5. **Who in 2006 was stripped of the Penrith Panthers captaincy following his drunken antics at a charity golf day?**
    a. Craig Gower
    b. Gareth Delve
    c. Gregor Townsend

6. **Who scored a hat-trick of tries in England's victory over Italy in 2005?**

   a. Steve Thompson
   b. Andy Hazell
   c. Mark Cueto

7. **The restaurant Sosban was opened in Llanelli in 2011. Who are the proprietors?**

   a. Scott Quinnell and Mark Taylor
   b. Stephen Jones and Dwayne Peel
   c. John Davies and Mefin Davies

8. **Who passed 500 Six Nations points in a match against Italy in February 2010?**

9. **Which former France captain replaced Marc Lièvremont as national coach in 2011?**

10. **Who was suspended for Wales' final match of the 2011 Six Nations following a confrontation with sports scientist Fergus Connolly?**

Round 37

1. **Who would you expect to see wearing green?**
   a. England
   b. Italy
   c. Ireland

2. **Durban, South Africa was the place of birth of which prop?**
   a. Duncan Jones
   b. Matt Stevens
   c. Tom Smith

3. **2010 saw the retirement of which 28-year-old scrum-half due to a succession of knee injuries?**
   a. Harry Ellis
   b. Dimitri Yachvili
   c. Gareth Cooper

4. **Following his 2010 debut, who scored 6 tries in his first 10 internationals?**
   a. Tavis Knoyle
   b. Ken Owens
   c. George North

5. **For which country did Diego Dominguez win 2 caps prior to making his Italian debut?**
   a. Romania
   b. Argentina
   c. Paraguay

6. **How many tries did Glenn Metcalfe score in his 40-game Test career?**

    a. 4

    b. 6

    c. 8

7. **Which footballer made an appearance in Rob Howley's 2005 testimonial team at the Millennium stadium?**

    a. Ian Rush

    b. Ally McCoist

    c. Ray Houghton

8. **Who was the former rugby league international that scored 6 tries in England's 2011 Six Nations tournament?**

9. **The winning country's emblem is placed as a handle on the lid of the Six Nations trophy. Where are the other countries emblems kept?**

10. **Which former outside-half was named as Scotland's attack coach in January 2009?**

Round 38

1. **Scotland prevented a 2011 Six Nations wooden spoon by winning their final match. Who was the opposition?**
    - a. Italy
    - b. France
    - c. England

2. **Yannick Nyanga, Gareth Thomas and William Servat have all played for which club side?**
    - a. Biarritz
    - b. Celtic Warriors
    - c. Toulouse

3. **Who was sin-binned on his Super 14 debut for the Sharks against the Crusaders in 2010, due to a high tackle on Dan Carter?**
    - a. James Hook
    - b. Andy Goode
    - c. Mirco Bergamasco

4. **Tony Buckley left Munster in 2011 to join which side?**
    - a. Cardiff Blues
    - b. Sale Sharks
    - c. Glasgow Warriors

5. **Who grabbed a last gasp try to give Wales a 31–24 victory over Scotland in 2010?**
    - a. Jamie Roberts
    - b. Stephen Jones
    - c. Shane Williams

6. **Who came second on ITV's 2010 reality series *71 Degrees North*?**

   a. Allister Hogg
   b. Gavin Henson
   c. Dan Luger

7. **England wing Lesley Vainikolo was qualified to play for which 2 other countries?**

   a. Samoa and Fiji
   b. Tonga and New Zealand
   c. Cook Islands and Japan

8. **In a match against England in 2010, who became the first Irishman to win 100 caps?**

9. **Who was suspended from the Wales squad in 2011 following an incident at a fast food restaurant in Cardiff?**

10. **Who captained England in their first Six Nations match, a 50–18 victory over Ireland at Twickenham in 2000?**

Round 39

1. **Which of the following has been capped in the back-row by Ireland?**
    a. Victor Costello
    b. Neil Back
    c. Geraint Lewis

2. **Who's the oldest from the following?**
    a. Denis Hickie
    b. Alessandro Troncon
    c. Leigh Davies

3. **Who was 2001 IRB Young Player of the Year?**
    a. Tommy Bowe
    b. Mirco Bergamasco
    c. Gavin Henson

4. **Which 44-times capped Welsh full-back retired in 2009 at the age of 29 through injury?**
    a. Kevin Morgan
    b. Rhys Williams
    c. Gareth Wyatt

5. **Who was the top points scorer in the inaugural Six Nations tournament?**
    a. Jonny Wilkinson
    b. Neil Jenkins
    c. Diego Dominguez

6. **From a broadcasting perspective, what was historical about Scotland's 27–22 victory over Wales in 2002?**
    a. First rugby match broadcast in high definition
    b. Last international match commentated on by Bill McLaren
    c. First Six Nations match not shown on terrestrial television

7. **In 2007, which Italian became the second overseas player to win the English Premiership Player of the Year award?**
    a. Marco Bortolami
    b. Martin Castrogiovanni
    c. Fabio Ongaro

8. ***Easter's Rising* is an autobiography released in 2011 about which Irish international?**

9. **Who was Wales' ever-present outside-half, scoring 57 points in their 2005 Grand Slam season?**

10. **What nationality is international referee Wayne Barnes?**

Round 40

1. **Flanker Richard Hill spent his entire career at which club?**
    a. Aberavon
    b. London Welsh
    c. Saracens

2. **Which of these is an Italian second-row?**
    a. Tommaso Benvenuti
    b. Mark Giacheri
    c. Ramiro Pez

3. **Who was the 2003 IRB Team of the Year?**
    a. England
    b. France
    c. Italy

4. **Who made 34 Scotland appearances from 1996 to 2002?**
    a. Martin Leslie
    b. Doddie Weir
    c. Mattie Stewart

5. *Getting Physical* **was an autobiography released in 2000 by which centre?**
    a. Scott Gibbs
    b. Will Greenwood
    c. James McLaren

6. **Whose last gasp try gave France a 17–20 victory over Ireland in 2007?**

     a. Yannick Jauzion
     b. Pierre Mignoni
     c. Vincent Clerc

7. **Sam Warburton had football trials with which club?**

     a. Cardiff City
     b. Manchester United
     c. Aston Villa

8. **What is the Calcutta Cup made from?**

9. **During Ireland's 14–13 victory over England in 2009, who received a yellow card for a mindless barge on Marcus Horan with 11 minutes of the game remaining?**

10. **Dan Baugh became a member of the Welsh coaching team in 2011. What nationality is he?**

Round 41

1. **Which country would you expect to see wearing white?**
    a. Italy
    b. Scotland
    c. England

2. **What nationality is 26-times capped Cameron Murray?**
    a. Scottish
    b. Irish
    c. French

3. **Who's the youngest of the following trio?**
    a. Dwayne Peel
    b. Simon Danielli
    c. Julien Bonnaire

4. **Castres Olympique signed which winger in 2011?**
    a. Shane Williams
    b. Max Evans
    c. Aled Brew

5. **Who on his Test debut was the famous victim of two showboating tackles by Gavin Henson in Wales' 11–9 win over England in 2005?**
    a. Matthew Tait
    b. Jonny Wilkinson
    c. Paul Sackey

6. **Back-row forwards Josh Sole and Aaron Persico were both born in which country?**

    a. USA
    b. Australia
    c. New Zealand

7. **Who scored both Irish tries in their 24–25 victory over Wales in 2003?**

    a. Denis Hickie
    b. Keith Gleeson
    c. Geordan Murphy

8. **Matt Dawson captained England 9 times between 1998 and 2001. Who previously was the last scrum-half to captain England?**

9. **Who became the Rugby World Cup sevens champions in 2009?**

10. **Who scored a brace of tries in England's 34–10 victory over France in 2009?**

Round 42

1. **Strokosch and Dickinson. What's their first name?**
   a. Dougie
   b. Richie
   c. Alasdair

2. **Who started all 5 of England's 2009 Six Nations matches at hooker?**
   a. Lee Mears
   b. Dylan Hartley
   c. George Chuter

3. **How did Elvis Vermeulen play an integral part in France winning the 2007 Six Nations?**
   a. National captain
   b. His end of the game try against Scotland gave France the required points difference over Ireland
   c. He kicked 3 penalties in the last 10 minutes against Wales to give the French victory at the Millennium Stadium

4. **At the age of 21, Jonny Wilkinson became England's record points scorer breaking the previous 396 points total. Who was the previous record holder?**
   a. Rob Andrew
   b. Jonathan Callard
   c. Jonathan Webb

5. **Which of these won 12 Welsh caps from 2000 to 2002?**

   a. Barry Williams
   b. Chris Wyatt
   c. Nathan Budgett

6. **Connor O'Shea was appointed director of rugby for which side in December 2009?**

   a. Munster
   b. Scarlets
   c. Harlequins

7. **Who was Italy's ever-present hooker in their first 3 seasons in the Six Nations?**

   a. Alessandro Moscardi
   b. Aaron Persico
   c. Giovanni Raineri

8. **With 796 points, who left the Ospreys in 2011 as their all-time leading marksman?**

9. **Which Irishman received the IRB 2001 distinguished service award?**

10. **With 31 tries in 55 caps, who was England's second highest try scorer on his retirement in 2006?**

Round 43

1. **Which prop won Test caps for Italy?**
   a. Ramiro Martinez
   b. Iestyn Thomas
   c. Jason Leonard

2. **Tom Voyce, Phil Vickery and Rory Lawson have all played for which side?**
   a. Cardiff Blues
   b. Gloucester
   c. Connacht

3. **Paolo Vaccari was an international full-back for which country?**
   a. France
   b. Italy
   c. Ireland

4. **Which of the following scored 8 tries in 25 Ireland appearances from 1998 to 2003?**
   a. Dion O'Cuinneagain
   b. Tom Tierney
   c. Justin Bishop

5. **Ian McGeechan spent 5 years in charge of which club during the 1990s?**
   a. Northampton Saints
   b. Swansea
   c. Melrose

6. **Wales' 29–12 win over France in 2008 was the dragons largest margin against the French since which year?**

      a. 1950

      b. 1960

      c. 1970

7. **How many caps did Andy Robinson win for England from 1988 to 1995?**

      a. 8

      b. 13

      c. 18

8. **Which former Ireland centre spent 4 years as North Otago coach, a period that included winning the Meads Cup in 2007?**

9. **Which 2 Wales players received yellow cards in their team's 12–16 victory over Ireland in 2008?**

10. **Which former winger was named French backs coach in 2007?**

Round 44

1. **Which of the following wingers played for Italy?**
   a. Shane Horgan
   b. Mark Jones
   c. Ludovico Nitoglia

2. **Former Eastenders actress Lucy Benjamin won the 2006 series *X Factor: Battle of the Stars*. Which rugby player did she defeat?**
   a. Matt Stevens
   b. Hugo Southwell
   c. Gethin Jenkins

3. **Which prop scored a try to help Wales to their only victory in the 2007 Six Nations, a 27–18 win against England?**
   a. Duncan Jones
   b. Rhys Thomas
   c. Chris Horsman

4. **Malcolm O'Kelly, Girvan Dempsey and Anthony Foley share which accolade?**
   a. Degrees from Oxford University
   b. Members of the IRUPA Hall of Fame
   c. All-Ireland hurling champions

5. **Who made his 200th Edinburgh appearance, against the Newport Gwent Dragons in September 2008?**
   a. Simon Webster
   b. Allan Jacobsen
   c. Geoff Cross

6. **Who scored 15 tries in a 48-cap career from 1996 to 2007?**

    a. Dafydd James
    b. Mark Jones
    c. Kevin Morgan

7. **Who made a try-scoring debut for Scotland A in 2009, having already made 36 senior appearances?**

    a. Dan Parks
    b. Hugo Southwell
    c. Sean Lamont

8. **Which Leinster Number 8 was the only player named in the Celtic League Team of the Year for 5 consecutive seasons from 2007 to 2011?**

9. **With a French record 380 points from 37 internationals, who set this tally from 1996 to 2001?**

10. **Who made a £2 million switch from Leeds Rhinos to Cardiff in 2001?**

Round 45

1. **Where was Mike Catt born?**
   a. Port Elizabeth, South Africa
   b. Maesteg, Wales
   c. Glasgow, Scotland

2. **Hugo Southwell played one-day cricket for which county in the 2000/01 season?**
   a. Hampshire
   b. Sussex
   c. Warwickshire

3. **Ireland recorded an 11–13 victory over Italy in 2011 thanks to a last gasp drop-goal. Who succeeded with the kick?**
   a. Jonathan Sexton
   b. Keith Earls
   c. Ronan O'Gara

4. **Who scored a brace of tries in France's 2011 defeat of Wales?**
   a. Lionel Nallet
   b. Julien Bonnaire
   c. Luc Ducalon

5. **Who is known as 'Alfie'?**
   a. Gareth Thomas
   b. Scott Gibbs
   c. Stephen Jones

6. **Following a 2001 debut, who reached 100 international points after just 9 Tests?**

    a. Chris Paterson

    b. Brendan Laney

    c. Duncan Hodge

7. **Whose last minute drop-goal gave Italy victory over Scotland in 2008?**

    a. Josh Sole

    b. Ezio Galon

    c. Andrea Marcato

8. **Martin Johnson captained England for the first time in 1998. Who was the last Leicester player to previously captain England?**

9. **Wales' 19–13 defeat of Ireland in 2011 was Warren Gatland's 36th game in charge making him Wales' longest serving in terms of matches. Whose 35-game record did he beat?**

10. **Which Scotland player was sent off against Wales in 2006 for lashing out at Ian Gough?**

Round 46

1. **Which of the following was an Italian international prop?**
    a. Giampiero de Carli
    b. Gethin Jenkins
    c. Euan Murray

2. **Who has created his own clothing range?**
    a. Mark Regan
    b. Imanol Harinordoquy
    c. Dwayne Peel

3. **Which centre had a father Dick who was also an England cap?**
    a. Mike Tindall
    b. Will Greenwood
    c. Andy Farrell

4. **Following his final international in 2003, who recorded 13 tries in a 70-cap career?**
    a. Kenny Logan
    b. Tony Stanger
    c. Derrick Lee

5. **Who was hospitalised following an attack on him outside a Cardiff nightclub in October 2008?**
    a. Mark Jones
    b. Alun Wyn Jones
    c. Mike Phillips

6. **Who was named ERC European Player of the Year for the 2010/11 season?**
    a. Jamie Heaslip
    b. Sean O'Brien
    c. Brian O'Driscoll

7. *Behind the Scrum* **was a 2004 autobiography by which scrum-half?**
    a. Andy Nicol
    b. Rob Howley
    c. Kyran Bracken

8. **Who made his final appearance for Scotland in 2005 having scored 6 tries in 61 games, making him his country's most capped prop?**

9. **Who were Wales' starting second-row partnership in their 2005 Grand Slam winning season?**

10. **England beat Wales to win an under-18s Grand Slam on the 12th of April 1997 in Narberth, Pembrokeshire. Who captained England for the first time in this encounter?**

Round 47

1. **Ronan O'Gara and Peter Stringer were half-back partners at which province before teaming up at international level?**
   a. Ulster
   b. Munster
   c. Connacht

2. **David Bory, Craig Moir and Justin Bishop appeared in the 2000 Six Nations competition. What position did they play?**
   a. Full-back
   b. Scrum-half
   c. Wing

3. **Carlo Festuccia, Andrea Lo Cicero, Santiago Dellapè and Andrea Masi have all played for which club?**
   a. Racing Metro
   b. Ebbw Vale
   c. Bristol

4. **Who retired as Ireland's most capped back-rower, after making his 65th appearance, against England in 2008?**
   a. Alan Quinlan
   b. Simon Easterby
   c. Anthony Foley

5. **Chris Paterson made his 88th Scotland appearance in 2008 making him his country's most capped player. Whose record did he break?**

    a. Scott Murray
    b. Stuart Grimes
    c. Scott Hastings

6. **Who came out of the international wilderness in 2007 to win a 70th and 71st cap, 4 years after his last?**

    a. Iain Balshaw
    b. Gareth Llewellyn
    c. Christian Califano

7. **Whose brace of tries helped Wales to a 23–10 defeat of Scotland in 2004?**

    a. Colin Charvis
    b. Rhys Williams
    c. Gareth Cooper

8. **Whose 24th championship try in 2011 equalled the record held by Ian Smith?**

9. **During the 2003 Six Nations, Diego Dominguez and Ramiro Pez were the two players to have started for Italy in which position?**

10. **Following Mike Ruddock's resignation, who took over as Wales' caretaker coach during the 2006 Six Nations?**

Round 48

1. **Scotland's Andrew Mower and Wales' Jason Jones-Hughes were both born in which city?**

   a. Edinburgh

   b. Sydney

   c. Newport

2. **Which former prop was made Scotland scrummaging coach in 2009?**

   a. Ricky Evans

   b. Massimo Cuttitta

   c. Victor Ubogu

3. **Who scored the only try in England's 17–9 win over France in 2011?**

   a. Ben Foden

   b. Tom Wood

   c. Andrew Sheridan

4. **Which Italian forward scored a drop-goal in his side's 2009 loss to Scotland?**

   a. Marco Bortolami

   b. Salvatore Perugini

   c. Sergio Parisse

5. **Who's the South African-born prop that won 70 French caps from 1999 to 2007?**

   a. Pieter de Villiers

   b. Jean-Jacques Crenca

   c. Jean-Baptiste Poux

6. **Who was the 2010/11 Celtic League Young Player of the Year?**

    a. Scott Williams
    b. Toby Faletau
    c. Dan Lydiate

7. **Who ended up playing for Ireland because Brian Ashton was watching David Corkery and was randomly told this player (who was also playing in the match) had a grandfather from Limerick?**

    a. Kevin Maggs
    b. John Kelly
    c. Eric Miller

8. **Who in 2009 became the first openly gay professional rugby union player?**

9. **Sale Sharks won the English Premiership for the first time in 2006. Who was their captain for the year?**

10. **During Scotland's 22–46 loss to Wales in 2005, who made a memorable try-scoring debut for the Scots?**

Round 49

1. **Which of the following was not an international full-back?**
   - a. Kevin Morgan
   - b. Carlo Cecchinato
   - c. Thomas Castaignède

2. **Which of the following was not an international back-rower?**
   - a. Scott Quinnell
   - b. Maurizio Zaffiri
   - c. Andrew Henderson

3. **Which English prop started all 5 games of their 2010 Six Nations?**
   - a. David Wilson
   - b. Dan Cole
   - c. Tim Payne

4. **In 2002, who was named IRB Player of the Year?**
   - a. Fabien Galthié
   - b. Brett Sinkinson
   - c. Budge Pountney

5. **Bryan Redpath became Scotland's most capped scrum-half in 2003. Whose 51-cap record did he break?**
   - a. Roy Laidlaw
   - b. Gary Armstrong
   - c. Andy Nicol

6. **Which telecommunication company became Irish shirt sponsor in 2006?**
    a. O_2
    b. Vodafone
    c. Orange

7. **What was significant about Wales' 2002/03 season?**
    a. First Six Nations whitewash
    b. A black shirt was used for the first time as an away strip
    c. The game with Italy was the first time a home match was not sold out in the championship since the war

8. **Who scored a hat-trick of tries in England's 59–12 victory over Italy in 2000?**

9. **Who scored 17 points as Italy defeated France 22–21 in 2011?**

10. **Which future Welsh coach made his international playing debut against Fiji in 1994?**

Round 50

1. **Who scored a hat-trick of tries as England beat Wales 44–15 in 2001?**
   - a. Dan Luger
   - b. Mike Catt
   - c. Will Greenwood

2. **Which future Italian coach won 56 French caps from 1981 to 1991?**
   - a. Pierre Berbizier
   - b. Serge Blanco
   - c. Denis Charvet

3. **Which Scottish back-row forward won his 50th cap in a 21–9 victory against Wales in 2007?**
   - a. Jon Petrie
   - b. Simon Taylor
   - c. Allister Hogg

4. **How many drop-goals did Neil Jenkins achieve over his Wales career?**
   - a. 0
   - b. 10
   - c. 15

5. **What did Christian Califano achieve in 2002?**
   - a. A record 4th Grand Slam
   - b. First French international to play Super Rugby with the Auckland Blues
   - c. 4 consecutive European Cup wins

6. **Nairobi, Kenya, was the place of birth of which English international?**
    a. Simon Shaw
    b. Neil Back
    c. Martin Corry

7. **Whose drop-goal helped Ireland to a 15–12 win over France in 2003?**
    a. David Humphreys
    b. Brian O'Driscoll
    c. Geordan Murphy

8. **With 75 appearances under his belt, who retired in 2005 as Scotland's most capped hooker?**

9. **Why was Mike Phillips' try controversial, as Wales beat Ireland 19–13 in March 2011?**

10. **Italy won their first match of the 2003 Six Nations 30–22. Who were the opposition?**

Answers

Round 1

1. c
2. b
3. c
4. c
5. a
6. a
7. b
8. Jason Leonard
9. David Humphreys
10. He's the father of Scottish internationals John and Martin Leslie

Round 2

1. a
2. a
3. b
4. c
5. b
6. a
7. c
8. New Zealand
9. Gordon Ross
10. France

Round 3

1. c
2. a

3. b
4. b
5. c
6. a
7. a
8. Lawson
9. Dwayne Peel
10. Delon Armitage

Round 4

1. a
2. c
3. a
4. b
5. c
6. b
7. a
8. Scotland and England
9. Andy Goode and Toby Flood
10. Ryan Jones

Round 5

1. c
2. b
3. a
4. b
5. a
6. c
7. a, with 4 tries
8. Karl Mullen
9. Serge Betsen
10. Gavin Henson

Round 6

1. b
2. a
3. c
4. b
5. b
6. a
7. b
8. Phil Vickery
9. Cardiff Arms Park, home of Cardiff RFC
10. Chris Paterson

Round 7

1. b
2. c, Hook in 2007, Heaslip in 2008, Ford in 2006
3. a
4. c
5. b
6. a
7. b
8. Nick Duncombe
9. John Kirwan
10. Ian McGeechan

Round 8

1. a
2. a
3. b
4. b
5. c
6. b
7. a

8. 4
9. Simon and Rory Best
10. Dwayne Peel

Round 9

1. c
2. b
3. a
4. b
5. c
6. a
7. c
8. Italy and France
9. Wales and France
10. Andy Farrell

Round 10

1. c
2. b
3. b
4. c
5. c
6. c
7. a
8. Jonathan Sexton
9. Robert Howley was Wales' last Five Nations captain, David Young was Wales' first Six Nations captain
10. England

Round 11

1. a
2. b

3. c
4. b
5. a
6. b
7. c
8. Chris Ashton
9. Bath
10. Gavin Henson

Round 12

1. c
2. b
3. a
4. c
5. a
6. c
7. a
8. Mick Galwey, David Humphreys and Keith Wood
9. David
10. Stephen Jones and James Hook

Round 13

1. c
2. a
3. b
4. c
5. a
6. b
7. c
8. Vincent Clerc
9. England
10. Sergio Parisse

Round 14

1. c
2. a
3. b
4. c
5. a
6. b
7. c
8. The Six Nations trophy
9. Rhys Ruddock, son of Mike
10. Garin Jenkins

Round 15

1. c
2. b
3. a, Kelly Jones is Stereophonics' lead singer
4. c
5. c
6. a
7. b
8. Ben Youngs
9. Ireland and England
10. Andy Powell and Tim Payne

Round 16

1. a
2. b
3. c
4. a
5. b
6. c
7. a

8. Will Carling
9. Keith Wood
10. Rugby union, 25 union caps, 20 league caps

Round 17

1. b
2. a
3. c
4. c
5. a
6. a
7. b
8. Declan Kidney
9. Gavin Henson
10. Matt Dawson

Round 18

1. a
2. b
3. c
4. b
5. a
6. a
7. c
8. The Calcutta Cup
9. Lawrence Dallaglio
10. Warren Gatland

Round 19

1. b
2. c
3. a

4. c
5. a
6. c
7. c
8. Gordon D'Arcy
9. Jamie Noon
10. Georgia

Round 20

1. b
2. a
3. c
4. b
5. c
6. a
7. a
8. Bill McLaren
9. Robert Howley
10. Martin Corry

Round 21

1. a
2. c
3. a
4. b
5. a
6. c
7. a
8. Michael Owen, in the 2005/06 season
9. Richard Hill
10. Sean Lamont

Round 22

1. b
2. a
3. c
4. a
5. c
6. b
7. a
8. Bernard Laporte
9. Ronan O'Gara
10. Jason Robinson

Round 23

1. c
2. c
3. a
4. b
5. b
6. c
7. a
8. Ryan Jones
9. Rob Kearney
10. South Africa

Round 24

1. b
2. a
3. c
4. a
5. b
6. a
7. c

8. Sam Warburton
9. Christian Califano
10. Chris Paterson

Round 25

1. b
2. c
3. b
4. b
5. a
6. c
7. c
8. Foot and Mouth disease in Britain
9. Austin Healey
10. Scott Macleod

Round 26

1. b
2. c
3. b
4. a
5. a
6. c
7. a
8. Eoin Reddan
9. Graham Henry
10. Matt Dawson

Round 27

1. c
2. b
3. b

4. c
5. b
6. b
7. a
8. Ulster
9. Mathieu Bastareaud
10. Simon Easterby

Round 28

1. a
2. a
3. b
4. b
5. c
6. c
7. a
8. Italy
9. Tony Marsh
10. Anthony Foley

Round 29

1. a
2. b
3. b
4. c
5. a
6. c
7. b
8. Wing
9. The Gaelic Athletic Association
10. Frank Hadden

Round 30

1. a
2. b
3. a
4. c
5. b
6. c
7. a
8. First Six Nations match at the Aviva stadium
9. Brynmor Williams
10. Eddie O'Sullivan

Round 31

1. c
2. b
3. c
4. b
5. c
6. a
7. b
8. Ben Cohen
9. Andy Craig
10. Brian O'Driscoll

Round 32

1. a
2. a, New Zealand
3. b
4. a
5. c
6. b
7. a

8. Matt Williams
9. Shane Williams
10. Harlequins

Round 33

1. a
2. c
3. b
4. a
5. c
6. a
7. b
8. Colin Charvis
9. Gloucester
10. Riki Flutey

Round 34

1. b
2. a
3. b
4. a
5. c
6. c
7. a
8. Magnus Lund
9. Steve Hansen
10. John Hayes

Round 35

1. a
2. c
3. b

4. b
5. c
6. c
7. a
8. Have been team captains on the BBC's *A Question of Sport*
9. Paul James, Richard Hibbard and Craig Mitchell
10. Max and Thom Evans

Round 36

1. c
2. a
3. b
4. a
5. a
6. c
7. b
8. Ronan O'Gara
9. Philippe Saint-André
10. Shaun Edwards

Round 37

1. c
2. b
3. a
4. c
5. b
6. a
7. b
8. Chris Ashton
9. In the plinth of the trophy
10. Gregor Townsend

Round 38

1. a
2. c
3. b
4. b
5. c
6. b
7. b
8. John Hayes
9. Mike Phillips
10. Matt Dawson

Round 39

1. a
2. b, Hickie and Davies born 1976, Troncon born 1973
3. c
4. b
5. a
6. b
7. b
8. Simon Easterby
9. Stephen Jones
10. English

Round 40

1. c
2. b
3. a
4. c
5. a
6. c

7. a
8. Silver rupees
9. Danny Care
10. Canadian

Round 41

1. c
2. a
3. a, Peel born in 1981, Danielli born in 1979, Bonnaire born in 1978
4. b
5. a
6. c
7. b
8. Richard Harding
9. Wales
10. Riki Flutey

Round 42

1. c
2. a
3. b
4. a
5. c
6. c
7. a
8. James Hook
9. Tom Kiernan
10. Will Greenwood

Round 43

1. a
2. b
3. b
4. c
5. a
6. a
7. a
8. Mike Mullins
9. Martyn Williams and Mike Phillips
10. Émile Ntamack

Round 44

1. c
2. a
3. c
4. b
5. b
6. a
7. c
8. Jamie Heaslip
9. Christophe Lamaison
10. Iestyn Harris

Round 45

1. a
2. b
3. c
4. a
5. a
6. b
7. c

8. Paul Dodge
9. Alan Davies
10. Scott Murray

Round 46

1. a
2. b
3. b
4. a
5. c
6. b
7. c
8. Tom Smith
9. Brent Cockbain and Robert Sidoli
10. Jonny Wilkinson

Round 47

1. b
2. c
3. a
4. b
5. a
6. c
7. b
8. Brian O'Driscoll
9. Outside-half
10. Scott Johnson

Round 48

1. b
2. b
3. a